by Kitt Winston
illustrated by Bill Melvin

SCHOOL PUBLISHERS

Printed in China

ISBN 10: 0-15-350506-0
ISBN 13: 978-0-15-350506-5

Ordering Options
ISBN 10: 0-15-350333-5 (Grade 3 Below-Level Collection)
ISBN 13: 978-0-15-350333-7 (Grade 3 Below-Level Collection)
ISBN 10: 0-15-357494-1 (package of 5)
ISBN 13: 978-0-15-357494-8 (package of 5)

3 4 5 6 7 8 9 10 985 12 11 10 09 08

On a clear night, the moon shines brightly. You might think that the moon gives off light, but it does not. Light from the sun reflects off the moon's surface.

Sometimes the moon looks like a large ball. Other times, it looks like a tiny sliver. Myths, or legends, were made up by early people to explain why the moon changes shape.

The early people of Greenland thought the sun goddess was chasing her brother, the moon god, across the sky. Greenland is an island in North America. The moon god ran so much that he forgot to eat. As days passed, he became thinner. Finally, the moon god had to stop and eat. He got bigger. The chase began all over again.

Today people understand why the shape of the moon changes. The changes are caused by the way the moon moves in space. The moon moves in two ways. It rotates, or spins around like a top. It takes the moon about twenty-nine days to rotate once. It also travels in a path around Earth called an orbit.

The different shapes of the moon are called phases. This is what the phases of the moon look like:

half moon

waxi

full

waxing gibbous

wani

The phases of the moon in order
are: full, waning gibbous, half moon,
crescent, new moon, waxing crescent,
half moon, waxing gibbous, and full.

rescent

new

half moon

ibbous

crescent

The moon takes about twenty-nine days to orbit around Earth. The sun always lights up half of the moon. We do not always see the lit-up half. When you see the lit-up half, the moon appears to be a full circle. This is called the *full moon.*

As the moon travels around Earth, we see less and less of the lit part. This is called the *waning moon*. Soon the lit-up part disappears from sight. This is called the *new moon*.

Then the moon starts to look lit up
again. The lit part that you see gets
bigger each day. This is called the *waxing
moon*. It takes about twenty-nine days for
all the phases. That's the same amount
of time it takes for the moon to make one
trip around Earth.

Starting in the 1950s, spacecraft were sent to study the moon. The spacecraft orbited the moon. Scientists learned more and more about the moon.

Then, on July 20, 1969, the first spacecraft carrying astronauts from Earth actually landed on the moon! People watched as a person walked on the moon's surface for the first time ever. It was on television!

The astronauts sent pictures of the moon back to Earth. The astronauts brought moon rocks back to Earth. From the rocks, scientists learned a lot about the moon. The rocks were evidence that scientists could study to learn how the moon might have been formed.

Scientists think the moon might once have been part of Earth. They think a large object from space hit Earth millions of years ago. The dust and ashes from Earth went into space and formed the moon. People have learned a lot about the moon since early times!

Think Critically

1. Why does the moon's shape appear to change in the sky?

2. How does the moon's shape change after the full moon?

3. Why do you think early people made up stories about the moon?

4. What question would you ask the first astronauts who landed on the moon?

5. What did you learn about the moon that surprised you? Explain.

Science

On the Moon Use a book or the Internet to find out more about when humans landed on the moon. Write a paragraph that tells what you learned.

School-Home Connection With a family member, look at the moon every night for one month. Draw a picture each night to show what it looks like. Then look at all the pictures to see how it changed.

Word Count: 512